A BEAUTIFUL MESS

By the same author:

Challenging Evil
Just Imagine: The Social Justice Agenda
The Liberating Truth
Boundless

A BEAUTIFUL MESS

How God re-creates our lives

Danielle Strickland

MONARCH
BOOKS

Oxford, UK, and Grand Rapids, Michigan, USA

Published by Monarch Books
an imprint of
Lion Hudson plc
Wilkinson House, Jordan Hill Road,
Oxford OX2 8DR, England
Email: monarch@lionhudson.com
www.lionhudson.com/monarch

ISBN 978 0 85721 594 9
e-ISBN 978 0 85721 595 6

First edition 2014

Acknowledgments
Unless otherwise stated Scripture quotations taken from The Message.
Copyright © by Eugene H. Peterson 1993, 1994, 1995, 1996, 2000, 2001,
2002. Used by permission of NavPress Publishing Group.
Scripture quotations marked NIV taken from the Holy Bible, New
International Version, copyright © 1973, 1978, 1984 International Bible
Society. Used by permission of Hodder & Stoughton, a member of the
Hodder Headline Group. All rights reserved. "NIV" is a trademark of
International Bible Society. UK trademark number 1448790.
Scripture quotations marked NLT are taken from the Holy Bible, New
Living Translation, copyright © 1996, 2004, 2007 by Tyndale House
Foundation. Used by permission of Tyndale House Publishers, Inc., Carol
Stream, Illinois 60188. All rights reserved.
Scripture quotations marked KJV from The Authorized (King James)
Version. Rights in the Authorized Version are vested in the Crown.
Reproduced by permission of the Crown's patentee, Cambridge University
Press.
Scripture quotations marked NRSV are from The New Revised Standard
Version of the Bible copyright © 1989 by the Division of Christian
Education of the National Council of Churches in the USA. Used by
permission. All Rights Reserved.

A catalogue record for this book is available from the British Library

Printed and bound in the United States, April 2016, LH37

To my Mom and Dad,

who endured the chaos

and were catalysts for

the beautiful mess of

my new life in

God's Kingdom.

Contents

Acknowledgments   9

Introduction   11

Chapter

1   Inevitable Chaos   13

2   Order Addicts Anonymous   23

3   Kicking at Darkness   43

4   Think Bigger   57

5   Holding the Landing   71

6   Seasons   81

7   Life: Mind-blowing Simplicity   91

8   Humanity   101

9   Rest: In Defiance of Slavery   111

Conclusion   119

Endnotes   123

Acknowledgments

Jill Rowe has edited this whole book, offered critique and content and designed the questions for reflection at the end of each chapter. Her commitment to leading people towards a creative divine design in their own lives is exemplary. I'm so thankful for her life and her valuable help in writing this book.

Introduction

When people ask me how my "work" is going I almost always reply, "It's a beautiful mess." I get a mixed response. Sometimes people measure success in stages of meticulous order. Others are gifted at crafting plans that are perfectly designed – with sub-points for specific ministry goals at the exact incremental stages for optimum growth. I've always envied lives that seem perfect. I've never had one.

My experience of life with God is messy. It's a mix of failure and success, courage and fear, faith and doubt. It's – well, a beautiful mess. If I were to tell the truth, since God invaded my life and welcomed me into a world of creative beauty, my whole life has been a beautiful mess. It's beautiful because it's a witness to the creative design of God's love in the here and now of our lives. My life doesn't look anything like it once did... I've been re-created by a designer who loves to recycle.

My life has taken a new shape. It's characterized by light and love; it's an expanding world that is constantly changing and yet I remain rooted in the foundations of God's love. It's filled with simple and complex truths that lead me to trust God and join Him in the invitation to bring heaven to earth.

It's a celebration that, even if it looks a little out of control – it's in the control of a loving God who has a plan.

So, this book is an invitation. You are invited to journey into God's creative plan to make a beautiful mess of your life and your plans. Like a master artist, He is ready to take the colours of your current life and craft them into a beauty that is beyond our comprehension.

This is how everything began, of course. With the original materials of a dark and shapeless void, the Hebrew creation story pictures an artist God who brings forth beauty from chaos. This story isn't used in this book as a scientific blueprint design, but as a window into the heart and strategies of a master designer. I'm amazed at how the original design has implications in the way He is still designing. Shaping in us new beginnings of beauty.

The heart of this book is to celebrate the ability of a grand artist to make a beautiful mess out of everything, and then to join Him in the process. Here's to living a re-created life.

Danielle Strickland
Summer 2014

Chapter One

Inevitable Chaos

We should start at the beginning. It's how it all began. The world was created out of chaos. This is one of the most fascinating parts of the story from the Hebrews. And it's a bit like all the other creation accounts from every other story told by people to try to explain why we exist. How it all started. *Chaos.* It's familiar in every single creation account on the planet and, if we are honest, it's also present in every one of our personal lives. Chaos.

It lurks around every corner, waiting to grab us by the ankles. It hides in the middle of every conversation, waiting to unsettle us and cause us to question. It nestles in the heart of every activist who dares to believe that the status quo sucks. And it bubbles under the surface in every boardroom where some people secretly remember the story of the founder that seems to have been lost in the pursuit of better margins, stronger profit, and happier shareholders.

What is "it"?

It's an invitation to rearrange everything. It's the starting place for creation. It's the bucket of paint that the artist can make into something beautiful. It's the possibility that things can change – for the better. Another name?

Chaos.

Encarta offers this definition of chaos:

1. a state of complete disorder and confusion

2. cha·os or Cha·os the unbounded space and formless matter supposed to have existed before the creation of the universe

3. the unpredictability inherent in a system such as the weather, in which apparently random changes occur as a result of the system's extreme sensitivity to small differences in initial conditions

(Encarta 2005)

For many people, chaos is a negative word. It is something that has to be righted; it is to be sorted out or perhaps hidden to create the illusion of order, even if it is only a temporary measure. Common understanding tells us that chaos is only ever a destructive force, quickly needing to be nailed down so that order can be brought to situations both personally and in our work scenarios. But what if there was a different way to understand chaos?

What if chaos was a good thing?

What if it was the root of all creativity?

What if it was the beginning of growth, personally and amongst the people and organizations we lead?

What if it was the seedbed of social change and transformation?

What if it loosed the chains of injustice?

What if it set captives free and actually began the process of repair in people's lives?

What if it did its thing, and everyone saw that it was "good"?

So here's the deal. Growth, whether personal or within an organizational structure, can only happen as a result of embracing chaos. Too many people have bought the idea that life is better without chaos, that unknowns are undesirable and the unexplainable is unnecessary.

C. S. Lewis, in *The Lion, the Witch and the Wardrobe* depicts Lucy standing at the wardrobe, with nowhere else to go. She is in the middle of an exciting game of hide-and-seek. There is literally just one place to hide and it is inside the wardrobe. She thinks it is like any other wardrobe, stuffed full of old coats and easily measurable in terms of size, and therefore a place of safety. She will stay in that musty space for as long as it takes. With her heart pounding, waiting to be found, she extends her hand out in front of her expecting to find the full extent of the depth of the wardrobe and so know just how far in she can hide. But instead of touching the "edge", she finds more "space", space that she can neither understand nor fathom. It literally makes no sense to her. It isn't how it is meant to be. But instead of running away from this void, she moves towards it, embracing the potential and fear of what might be found there. And to her delight, so begins the story of a whole new world.

There is an old Hebraic story describing the creation of the world. It begins with Yahweh moving over the chaos and void.

"God created the heavens and earth – all you see, all you don't see. Earth was a soup of nothingness, a bottomless emptiness, an inky blackness. God's Spirit brooded like a bird above the watery abyss".[1]

The imagery is potent: of God above the chaos, yet strongly present in it. The story continues through a series of phases: first comes LIGHT, then EXPANSE, then LAND, then SEASONS, then LIFE, then REPRODUCTION and finally REST.

And this story gives us a divine pattern to the way of things. We call this a beautiful mess. It's how God re-creates life. It looks like this:

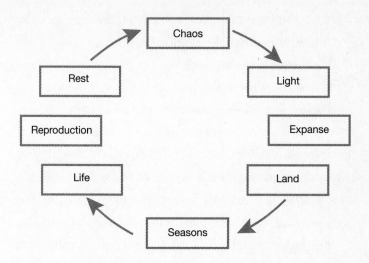

What God creates is very good. That's how He put it. Like an artist who can't wait to show you what has emerged – like a mum and dad who are beaming as they hold up their little baby; like a gardener, stepping back with dirt under his fingernails to admire the sheer beauty of the created – very good indeed.

But it all begins with chaos.

At the very core and heart of the story is this unmanageable, beautiful, wonderful disorder out of which everything else comes. The point is that without the chaos, nothing else would have been born from it.

17

Creation would not have been given breath.
It is all because of the chaotic beginning
that order is made possible.
It was never the other way round!
Chaos first, always.

But we live in a culture that seeks to hide chaos. To admit that there is chaos in your life is a sign of weakness and failure. To not have it together, or to not have life seemingly sorted, at least on the outside, is to have somehow dropped the Holy Grail.

For many people, this results in quite a significant cover-up job, where lives appear to have a serene veneer masking unanswered questions, swathes of self-doubt and stunted personal growth.

The truth is that we are afraid of things we can't control. Chaos is uncontrollable – by its definition you can't predict what it will do or what effect it will have. This makes those of us who fear change and loss of control very uneasy. We like to know what we are facing and we like to control our environment. But chaos doesn't care about our fear. Chaos enters and turns everything upside down. Perhaps this is the right treatment for those of us who think we hold it all together; those of us who are afraid of change and afraid of circumstances outside of our control. This "mess" called chaos reorders things in our lives... shifting and changing our values and reminding us of what's most important.

I've been intrigued by the current popularity of zombies. What is it about zombies and the possibility of apocalypse that has captured the attention of a generation? I've been asking people what they think and I've been surprised by the results. Most of the people I've asked suggest that underneath the extreme controls of our modern world we wonder about deeper things. For example, what really matters. If all the shiny controlled neatness of our lives were taken away, what would be left? What would really matter?

What about the leading of programmes and initiatives? The same is true. To run a business that is neat and tidy, that is efficient but strangely similar to what it has been for the past x years is hailed by many as a good place to work and a mark of success. But a closer look informs you that life has been drained out of the organization. It could be merely going through the motions and creativity has been successfully subdued in honour of predictable and controllable order.

What if the pursuit of order has created a love of the status quo and has removed the passion for justice? What if we have made a friend of comfort instead of change and as a result removed ourselves from the responsibility that demands that we fight for change to happen? Wasn't it out of chaos that apartheid ended and the Iron Curtain fell?

This book is concerned with rediscovering chaos as the root of growth for us personally, organizationally and as the required instigator of transformation in local communities. It is about our ability to embrace this dynamic, to not shy away from it and to journey alongside others as they discover what it means in their own lives. Living is about functioning effectively with the unknown, about finding the path to the next landing point without necessarily knowing the destination or the route to take in advance. It is about being comfortable in what feels chaotic and recognizing the huge creativity and beauty of that place.

As we begin this journey, the words of Thomas Merton, an American Catholic who was part of the Order of the Strict Cistercians, provide us with sustenance for the outrageous chaos-marked adventure ahead.

> **My Lord God, I have no idea where I am going.**
> **I do not see the road ahead of me.**
> **I cannot know for certain where it will end.**
> **Nor do I really know myself,**
> **and the fact that I think I am following your will**
> **Does not mean that I am actually doing so.**
> **But I believe that the desire to please you does in**
> **fact please you.**
> **And I hope I have that desire in all that I am doing.**
> **I hope that I will never do anything apart from**
> **that desire.**

And I know that if I do this
you will lead me by the right road though I may
know nothing about it.
Therefore will I trust you always though I may
seem
to be lost in the shadow of death.
I will not fear, for you are ever with me,
and you will never leave me to face my perils alone.[2]

Questions

- What is my first response to the thought of chaos? What does this response show me about myself?

- How do I feel about unanswered questions and unresolved situations both personally and in the work context?

- When did I last experience chaos? What came as a result of this experience?

- How do I as a friend help others understand situations of chaos?

Chapter Two

Order Addicts Anonymous

Chaos and Order are not enemies, only opposites.

Richard Garriott

Chaos is simply the beginning of the process, a process that is cyclical. It has a close friend called "order". They dwell in near communion, sometimes at peace and sometimes in tension. But always near. And there is a beauty in that relationship. It is as if they are mutually dependent, as if one necessarily flows from the other. It's as if there was a glimpse of the divine in this chaotic ordering.

So what is "order":

1. to command somebody to do something

2. to give an instruction for something to be done

3. to give an instruction for something to be provided, for example, food in a restaurant or merchandise from a manufacturer or supplier

4. to arrange items in a particular way, especially in the sequence in which they are to be dealt with

5. to put things into a neat, well-organized state or into the required state

(Encarta, 2005)

I was travelling with a friend on the subway in downtown Toronto – we were heading to a much-loved hangout. Suddenly on the train my friend burst out into one of her "Musical" favourites. If it helps you to imagine, it was the lead song from the musical *Hair* (a classic). She was fully animated – shyness was not her problem. She wasn't much of a student, having just been expelled from school, but she was certainly an actress! She performed as though on Broadway.

It was a spectacular production. I loved so many things about that incident. I loved her abandon. I loved her zeal for life. I loved her freedom. But most of all, I loved the way it created chaos in a seemingly mundane and boring subway car. Suddenly everything in the car changed. A number of people stood up and got off at the next stop. Others laughed, albeit quite nervously; some tightened their grip on their poles and hung on. Several tried to ignore the show but couldn't help taking a peek. I was a bit worried for one particular elderly lady. It looked like her heart might not hold up – the sheer shock of this "Musical moment" on a normal subway ride seemed to throw the whole train into madness. It was wild and totally chaotic.

There is something fun about that kind of chaos. It is the kind that interrupts the mediocrity of normalcy. It is the sort of chaos that disrupts the status quo of the everyday.

It seems that there is a common link in all of the stories depicting the origins of chaos; chaos gives birth to something. *Chaos is inevitably linked to the creation of new things.* From a faith perspective, it is out of the "chaotic void" that God speaks life. It is from chaos that everything else is born. It is chaos as a parent, as a mother, as a beginning, as a start to everything else. There can be something refreshing about the disordering of life. There is something fantastic about order when it is birthed from chaos.

> **One of the advantages of being disorderly is that one is constantly making exciting discoveries.**
>
> A. A. Milne

But the reality is that just as we have a slightly jaded and disrespectful view of chaos, we have, at times, an overwhelming fascination with order. For a long time we held on to modernity's optimistic view of rational order, believing that it would make society better. But the reality of the unfolding world events over the past century simply doesn't reflect that belief. Communism, arguably one of the most "ordered" movements ever imagined by humanity, left a lot to be desired when it broke open and people began to see the sham behind the wall and the Iron Curtain. The twentieth century was full of well-ordered genocides, wars, poverty and general chaos, all of which took place in a systemic and orderly context. So, while the modern world has been crying "order" as the answer to the great problem of chaos, it has not answered well. Indeed, it has left us with plenty of theory but without the desired outcome.

On a personal level as well, the idea that ordered lives are fulfilled lives is at odds with both the external and internal results of our generation. Depression, suicide, hopelessness, and addiction – all of them are on the rise. The need to "control" chaos (at least in the light of a modern understanding of it) brings with it a compartmentalization of life. We become less integrated and therefore less whole. But too much order generates its destruction. If instead of clinging desperately to order we allow God to set the priorities, then the divine can and does speak a different kind of order into existence that promises permanent and lasting meaning for us personally and in the work that we are a part of.

Instead of feeling threatened by the label of "chaotic and disorderly", the artist Jackson Pollock embraced the idea as a badge of honour for any artist. "There was a reviewer," Pollock said, "who wrote that my pictures didn't have a beginning or an end. He didn't mean it as a compliment, but it was. It was a fine compliment." Artists aren't primarily concerned with order. They are concerned with beauty, freedom, expression, emotion, paradox, dissonance, and colour. Not order. Order speaks of a scholar who must put together a thesis that is controlled, rational, ordered, reasonable, and factual. An artist is interested in something other than fact. Art is experienced. It is not a critical path analysis.

We need to view the relationship between chaos and order with fresh eyes and new understanding as we grow in and through this messy and sometimes painful dynamic.

The difficulties associated with this transitional experience of moving from human order to divine chaos are various and multi-layered.

It requires us to live within what could be called the "chaotic void". It forces us to find the capacity and desire to sit within that chaos and take note of what is happening there. Perhaps God is speaking. Maybe there are the beginnings of change bubbling under the surface. Perhaps justice is emerging in a local community context. Perhaps the questions associated with the chaos are bringing with them a new-found energy to find solutions to previously unexplored or understood problems on a multitude of levels.

I have a friend who caught her husband in an affair. It was a horrible experience. It rocked her world. Everything about her existence was thrown into chaos. What proceeded was more chaos – anger, despair, an ugly divorce, and isolation. It seemed like a dead end. But as she sat in that chaotic void, she started to look for God and something began to emerge. She saw light dawning on a new beginning. She began to follow the light and it led her to Africa. She started using her gifts to help orphans and widows, and what is emerging from her chaos is something so beautiful and rich and different than her life would have been. She now has the ability to look back and see that even the chaos was an opportunity to see God's order emerge in her life. Even the darkness helped her moved towards God's Divine Order for her life. It's really fascinating because as a little girl she used to dream of being a missionary. Somehow in the ordering of her life that never happened. It wasn't until chaos reordered her life that it was even possible.

A good friend leads an international campaign focused on bringing an end to people trafficking (www.stopthetraffik.org). Every step of the journey of that campaign has been steeped in chaos and messiness. It has been exhausting and pure hard graft. There have been many achievements but there are still some huge mountains to climb. But the Stop the Traffik campaign has needed to be chaotic because it has had to unsettle the status quo. It has had to raise its voice to shout for the millions of silent, oppressed trafficking victims around the globe. Because it has existed in that chaotic space it has been able to bring more of the freedom and justice it has been calling for. And that is where order emerges from chaos.

Learning to swim is at the same time one of the most terrifying, exciting and thrilling experiences you can have as a child. You cling on for dear life to the rail running along the edge of the pool knowing that when you let go there are literally only two things that can happen – sink or swim. With a heart beating so loudly you can hear it in your own head and with the biggest gulp of air you can muster, you let go and make rapid movements with your arms and legs thrashing around creating minor tidal waves as you begin to swim. The feeling moves from fear to elation, and it is all because you let go of the handrail. You let go.

We have to learn to let go in this transition from human chaos to Divine Order. The temptation is to hold on tight to what has been previously, the old way and the old rhythm of things. The old often feels more comfortable and somehow safer; it is what we have always known. But that certainly doesn't make it better. To create a new order out of the chaos we have to let go and abandon ourselves to the possibility of the new, bringing with us the deep learning of our journey to guide us.

The truth is that our finest moments are most likely to occur when we are feeling deeply uncomfortable, unhappy, or unfulfilled. For

it is only in such moments, propelled by our discomfort, that we are likely to step out of our ruts and start searching for different ways or truer answers.

M. Scott Peck

Courage is required in the transition from chaos to order. But it's not the courage we are used to. We are used to courage that is active; the stereotypical superhero who saves the day.

The kind of courage that God requires of us is to believe. It's to hang on to faith in the midst of circumstances that feel like a dead end. It's to know that the light is coming – that the dawn will break – that God really is enough. God is not going to leave us alone. That's the kind of courage it requires.

It's much harder than rushing in to fix everything that's wrong. It's the courage to wait for God. It's the courage to admit that you can't fix it. That not everything is fixable. That maybe there is something deeper at work and we need to sit here a while to find out what. It's the courage to not be in control. To let God lead.

This is a deep courage that few have the nerve to live. But it is always the invitation God extends to us. This is the first story of the invitation to partner with God through a man named Abraham. His story is a strange one to us because in the Bible God says there is no one else like him. He pleased God and was His friend because he had faith. He believed God. The reason this is extraordinary is because Abraham had *every reason* not to. Everything God told Abraham to do seemed crazy – chaotic. His whole life was turned upside down (many times). God told him to leave everything familiar to him. His home, his people, and his gods. He told him that he would make him a nation of priests and it would begin through a promised son. This was especially difficult to believe because Abraham was married to a barren woman. No son, no people, no nation. It was a period of divine chaos, a reshifting of Abraham's foundations. Normal was traded in and chaos took its place. But what Abraham did was let go of his need for information and control, and let God take the lead. And right when it seemed like darkness was all there was to be, light came and God's order emerged. A son was born. A promise was kept. A people emerged, a nation even. It was a Divine Order that included the blessing of the entire earth.

Who would have thought that a little tribal chief in the desert believing God despite the circumstances could have that kind of effect on the world? I wonder what kind of effect our embracing of chaos and waiting for God's order could have on ours?

This process inevitably leads us to doubt. And many people of faith mistakenly think that doubt is a enemy. I believe it to be a friend. A friend is someone who wants to know more. And doubt wants just that. It's in the middle of doubt and fear that faith actually arises; when we choose to believe God despite what we feel or can't explain. It's that faith that pleases God because He knows our deepest desires and our willingness to trust Him.

There is a need to apply this same principle of taking courage in situations of community as well. Leaders may have brought the people or organization they lead to a point which seemed steady and "safe" but where now all feels chaotic and is marked by messiness. Leadership may feel more like holding on for dear life in the middle of a storm than a position of untouchable optimism. Undoubtedly for a leader that is a lonely and dark place, deep with questions of self-doubt concerning the lack of right qualifications to really be the leader, and a fear of "what might happen if we don't make it". The skill of a leader is to recognize this as "chaos", part of the cyclical process of chaotic order, and the source of creativity and growth. To begin to see the potential pattern and order that can emerge, there is a need to get a view of the bigger picture and gain a proper perspective.

> **I have a great belief in the fact that whenever there is chaos, it creates wonderful thinking. I consider chaos a gift.**
>
> Septima Poinsette Clark

> **God, make a fresh start in me, shape a Genesis week from the chaos of my life.**
>
> King David, Psalm 51:10

If we desire to grow personally, if we want our lives to count, if we long to start things that matter and are about life in its fullness, and earnestly want to go after the things that really make life worth living, if we want our communities to be changed, then we might need to start asking for chaos to visit our lives, to visit our businesses and companies, our schools, churches, organizations and society. We might need a little disorder for a new beginning. After all, chaos is part of the Divine Order of life.

I remember being in Russia right after the collapse of the Soviet Union. One of my jobs was to coordinate youth and children's activities at a new church in Moscow. We announced Sunday school one week and the next week there were 300 children. It was chaos.

Eventually we put together a camp and held it at a facility that used to be a Soviet youth camp. One of the key items on a camp schedule is the flag raising at the start of the day. We had all gathered around the flagpole on the first morning of the camp when it dawned on us that we were missing two key ingredients in a flag raising ceremony; a flag and an anthem. Because of the collapse of the Soviet Union the flag was no longer considered a friendly sight, and the anthem – well, it was unusable. It was filled with rhetoric that had now proven to be blatant lies. I asked my good friend and translator Olga how bad it could be – and she said it was worse than I could imagine.

What a difficult place to be in; the people had been fed a lot of lies to keep the outside looking good – but all the while the inside was not matching up. Jesus called this the "whitewashed tombs" syndrome when He rebuked the Pharisees in Matthew's Gospel (23:27). And I think, essentially, that's where we have arrived in our current culture.

The promise of modernity, the well-ordered, scientific, carefully controlled consensus that dominated most of the twentieth century, was that it answered everything. But what it really answered were external questions such as technological advance, intellectual pursuit, reason, and progress. The internal things, the things that keep us up at night – do our lives matter, are we loved, what is the meaning of life? – that's where the modern age failed us.

My friend Olga and I continued our conversation about the bankruptcy of her culture later. I asked her if she was really angry with her leaders and government for lying to her – even teaching her things that were untrue. She replied with wisdom well beyond her twenty years. She said, "The leaders may have lied to the Russian people, but the people chose to believe them."

And that really is the crux of it. It is sometimes simply easier to believe that things are ordered, reasonable, predictable, and completely under our control. But the reality of our world is that it is unpredictable, often random and unreasonable, chaotic and completely out of our control. And that's when modernity's promises run empty and its progress reports run dry.

The church does the exact same thing. We try to promote a God of equations: if you give – He will bless; if you obey – He will lead you to successful places; if you live well – you will get to heaven. Religion will assure you that an ordered life is a secure one. But there are way too many stories in the Bible and in church history to suggest that that simply isn't true. God's promises are true and He will bring an order to our lives – but it isn't always the order that makes human sense. From prophets to priests to disciples to Jesus Himself – their lives seemed a chaotic mess except for God, who makes sense of it all.

The truth is that we cannot maintain "human order style" control in a postmodern world, no matter how hard we try. Embracing chaos is less a choice than a survival tool. And it is more than that, too. It's also about matching the internal realities of our nature and our world with the external measures of success; it's about *being truthful AND deep*. It's not just about knowledge; it's truth that penetrates, truth that matters, truth that isn't afraid to ask hard questions and risk failure. Truth that would rather embrace honest chaos than continue to whitewash the tombs of our culture so we die looking good. It's really about allowing the chaos to show a bit, and even enjoy it.

A lump of clay needs to be shaped and moulded by a potter. It cannot become what it can be without the skilful and careful gracious hands of the master craftsman. In the Bible, the prophet Jeremiah uses the image of a potter in reference to God shaping our lives, "Like clay in the hand of the potter".[3] Out of chaos, a beautiful order is formed, an order that moves us in the right direction, an order that enables us to become more fully who we were created to be, individually and corporately.

> **God made my life complete**
> **when I placed all the pieces before him.**
> **When I got my act together,**
> **he gave me a fresh start.**
> **Now I'm alert to God's ways;**
> **I don't take God for granted.**
> **Every day I review the ways he works;**
> **I try not to miss a trick.**
> **I feel put back together,**
> **and I'm watching my step.**
> **God rewrote the text of my life**
> **when I opened the book of my heart to his eyes.**

Psalm 18:20–24

Messiness: A lifestyle

One of the major implications in embracing chaos as lifestyle is the inevitable unpredictability of journey and destination.

This is difficult in many organizations. In order to start something new, you probably need to fill out a fourteen-page programme proposal. This is a good idea. It helps you sort out purpose and goals and process. Here's the problem. If you are "embracing chaos" and feel you should position yourself within the messiness of lives, communities, and cities to watch God begin establishing order and then join in with that, it's difficult to explain this in the proposal. The proposal asks you to give a plan. The plan needs to include goals. These goals are to be measurable and reasonable. (This is all sounding good and probably quite familiar, right?) But how can you set goals and purpose when you are plunging into chaos? Is chaos measurable? And if so, how do you depict embracing chaos on a chart?

For example: I'm aiming at getting intricately involved with ten messy people (part one of programme proposal). Then I plan to watch what God says, and join in creating new life from the chaos (part two of programme proposal). How do you measure that (big problem in programme proposal)? What's the timeline for a new creation (no idea for programme proposal)? And it gets even messier. If I'm aiming at relationship instead of function (that is the chaos instead of order), then how do I measure my effectiveness?

Difficult. Here's where it gets even messier. How do I measure what's work and what's life?

I remember my running partner from years back. We became great friends (and our running came a long way as well). Over a long time, she grew to know Jesus and really got excited about her faith. It was quite an energizing season. In the beginning of our relationship she asked me a pointed question. In the middle of a run, out popped, "Am I a project?"

I feigned shock. We talked it through and worked it out. However, the question stuck with me. It was true that I was involved in community initiatives and life in order to create relationships with people. And so I wanted my relationships to represent Christ well. I hoped that my life might be a light to help dispel the darkness of unbelief and meaninglessness in theirs. Was my running partner a friend or a project? Good question. So I pondered it for a while.

Of course, I told her she wasn't a project, and meant it. But deep within my heart I started to really question my own motives and how I worked from authentic relationships to church expansion. Somewhere in my ponderings I stumbled upon the answer. It was both and neither all at the same time. It was simply this – messy. Boundaries overlapped. She was both a friend and a project but not even at the same time and also all at once. She was my friend no matter what happened between her and Jesus, but she was my project in that I had something (Someone) she needed to know, and I needed to tell her.

She was my running partner and helped me tremendously in both body and spirit. Her honesty was infectious and her training gruelling. I started understanding for the first time that the truth of it was that our relationship was in chaos. There was no definition that would fit. It was disordered. God figured it out. He brought life and spoke the word into our midst and we began to see a Divine Order emerge that was lasting and true. But it was messy. The big implication of embracing chaos is to choose the mess. David says it like this:

> When my soul is in the dumps, I rehearse
> everything I know of you,
> From Jordan depths to Hermon heights,
> including Mount Mizar.
>
> Chaos calls to chaos,
> to the tune of whitewater rapids.
> Your breaking surf, your thundering breakers
> crash and crush me.
>
> Then God promises to love me all day,
> sing songs all through the night!
> My life is God's prayer.

> Psalm 42:6–8

Embracing chaos (or entering into the messiness of others' lives) is a necessary precursor to God doing something new in people's lives (and probably in ours, as well).

> **The reason the mass of men fear God, and at bottom dislike Him, is because they rather distrust His heart, and fancy Him all brain like a watch.**
>
> Herman Melville

> **Man is not an arithmetical expression; he is a mysterious and puzzling being, and his nature is extreme and contradictory all through.**
>
> Fyodor Dostoevsky

The best model for embracing chaos as a tool for establishing God's order into our lives and into our relationship is the first time He does it!

Genesis 1–3 creation is a blueprint for Divine Order. It starkly contrasts our version of order:

In approach: It emerges from within, rather than being imposed from without. This is the chaotic part to us. Often we have a set goal we are hoping to achieve. God is creating from within. What if we looked for the beautiful moments of creation within our relationships, rather than imposing them before our relationships grow? What if we looked for God's incredible ability to create beauty and meaning in the midst of the people we are already with, instead of thinking there are perfect people somewhere for us to find?

In process: God's order is characterized by symbiotic interdependence. Every stage is connected to the other. Rather than neat, tightly aligned stages of growth, every stage is interdependent. They are deeply connected – organically woven. It makes separating them impossible and the risks are much bigger as a result. What happens in a ministry or a relationship when one part gets unhealthy? It means every part is affected. And this is messy business. Many ministries and lives are segregated in the hopes of not infecting each other. This has an upside (control, for one thing) but it also has a downside. Every part of our lives should be integrated... that's what roots us in a foundation of authentic growth. Without this authenticity we can easily lose ourselves. The risks are present – but the reward is sweet.

In character: Each stage is catalytic. Every part of the creation account has its own creative power. Every part of it is good (God makes sure He says this out loud so we won't miss it). No matter what part is your favourite, it's all good. And it's all creative and life-giving. The light, the expanse, the water, the animals, the plants, the seasons... every single thing is a catalyst for more beauty, more life.

Every stage is infused with creative order.

Questions

- What is my perspective right now on the chaos I am experiencing?

- Do I see a pattern emerging?

- What am I hearing about the way ahead?

- To what extent am I clinging on amidst the chaos?

- What do I need to let go of that may be preventing me from embracing the chaos?

- Do I need to ask someone to help me see and understand the new order that is emerging?

- Am I too ready to stay with chaos and not do the hard work associated with developing and embracing order?

Chapter Three

Kicking at Darkness

You've got to kick at darkness until it bleeds daylight.

Bruce Cockburn

A few years ago I had some laser eye surgery. It was a very interesting experience that certainly isn't for the fainthearted. It includes having your retina reshaped so that the image your eye sees is clearer. It's unpleasant in that you remain conscious throughout. Think taped-open eyelids, frozen eyeballs and lasers reshaping the back of your eye. Ouch. At one point during the surgery, I remarked that the experience felt very similar to one I had seen Tom Cruise go through in the movie *Minority Report*. Everyone agreed. The results of the surgery have been impressive. I no longer have to wear glasses or contact lenses. I can see clearly now.

A friend of mine is a surgeon who spends a lot of time working amongst the poor and marginalized in the developing world. He recently decided to learn how to perform eye surgery so that he could make it possible for many people in such communities and countries to regain their sight. And each time he returns from a period of doing such work, he is full of stories of people being able to see again. Their joy is uncontainable. Their vision has literally been flooded with light. And darkness has been dispelled.

In the Hebraic story of creation, on the first day, the first stage of Divine Order springs out of the chaos of the deep.

> **Now the earth was formless and empty, darkness was over the surface of the deep, and the Spirit of God was hovering over the waters. And God said, "Let there be light," and there was light. God saw that the light was good, and he separated the light from the darkness.**

Genesis 1:2–4 (NIV)

Revelation, the bringing of light, is the first part of the journey necessary to establish order out of chaos. It's the first part of the creative process.

God said, "Let there be light". Revelation is the first tool required to establish beauty. It is the initial action of creating something from nothing.

Starting with light is essential in creating an enduring order. There is a certain divine strength to light. We do not put blinds up to protect ourselves from the darkness. Light powerfully penetrates. Darkness is afraid of the light. "… light shines in the darkness, and the darkness can never extinguish it".[4]

Saul is a highly significant character you can read about in the New Testament. He spent his time persecuting Christians as he travelled through the land seeking to restore order to the chaos they had caused. But it was then that he ran into something that stopped him in his tracks, turned his world upside down and changed everything – and that was light. It was a piercing, wild, bright, and blinding light: "As he was approaching Damascus on this mission, a light from heaven suddenly shone down around him".[5] This was the first step to creating Divine Order in Saul's life. What follows looked and must have felt like complete chaos: darkness, a revelation of Jesus, and a collapse of an old worldview. Saul was submerged in personal chaos.

But God used light to spark a chaos from which He could craft Divine Order.

That's a loaded sentence. Let me repeat: God used light to spark a chaos. This chaos created a starting place for God to re-establish His creative design for Saul's life. Light is a powerful tool in the hands of a loving God.

Saul morphs into Paul – Acts 13:9 – and charges through the New Testament armed with physical sight *and* revelation to establish Divine Order. The thing about Paul's transformation is that his ability to grasp God's revelation is remarkable. Even the original disciples find it hard to keep up with him. When they think they should slow down for fear of offending the Jews, Paul rebukes them and reminds them that the gospel is for the whole world. This from the man who was killing Christians to protect the Jewish faith. Divine revelation makes us into a people who can "see". We can understand things from God's perspective. We have the ability to see differently.

I spent some time journeying around Israel. My dad joined me there and we decided that it was the perfect opportunity to climb Mount Sinai. But we didn't want to pay tourist rates and have to experience the journey on the back of a donkey. So we sought out a local taxi driver and, accompanied by an Englishman who also didn't want to pay through the nose, we were driven to the base of Mount Sinai. It was pitch dark and the three of us couldn't see our hands in front of our faces. The taxi driver literally dropped us off and sped away. We had clearly only bought a one-way ride!

For a moment the three of us tried to get accustomed to the darkness. I suggested that what we could really do with was a torch. Right then our very new English friend reached into his pocket and pulled out a pen with a special light fitting on the end. Believe me, it sounds more impressive than it was. The power of the beam increased our ability to see in front of us by about 4 cm. Did I mention it was pitch black?

So there we were, armed with a highly ineffective torch and nothing else apart from a large climb ahead of us. At the top of Mount Sinai we knew we would meet a monk whose job was to make tea for those who made the pilgrimage.

Together we began our climb, scrambling over rocks but only seeing what was right in front of our faces. At one point two eyes confronted me in the darkness. My initial fears were quickly calmed when, with the aid of the pen torch, it became apparent that this was not in fact a relative of the sabre-toothed tiger family, looking for supper, but was actually a roaming cow.

A couple of hours later we arrived at the top and were greeted by the monk and an incredible sunrise, as light broke in the darkness. To call it an incredible sunrise is to understate the experience. We saw the glow of the sun emerge from the horizon. It looked like it was setting the desert hills on fire. The glow itself (before the sun even really had risen) was overwhelmingly beautiful – bringing warmth and light at the same time. The glow spread, lighting the sand with fire, making the desert a glowing river of gold. As the sun rose, the depths of our souls were touched with warmth and light. The sheer power of that light was overwhelming.

Below us we could see the winding path that those tourists who paid would have made on the backs of donkeys. It seemed to be a much safer way to come. I then turned and took a look at the route we had taken. To be honest I was a bit surprised. It was only in the daylight that I could see just how treacherous it had been. There were holes, and boulders, and many other obstacles that would have worried even the keenest climber. Sometimes when we can see where we are going we do not move forward because we are afraid of all the obstacles we can see ahead. The darkness can sometimes be a friend in these situations. And the light we need to continue our journey is "just enough" for us to put one foot in front of the other. But all along the way we know the dawn will rise.

But we had made our ascent. We had just enough light to enable us to make each step towards our goal. Yes, we could have waited for daylight but we wanted to see the sunrise from the summit. The light came as we moved forward; with each step it became brighter, and each step was towards our destination. The climb was more difficult than I had imagined (as are most of our journeys) but it was worth it. The effect the moment on the summit had on me was that I'd do it again, and again, and again. To see the sun emerge and the light spread and the warmth inside my own bones… it was all enhanced by the journey in the darkness, not diminished by it. And this is the point of our beautiful mess. The darkness is real, the climb is treacherous and the conditions are never perfect, but the summit is worth it. The moments when we can see God's light emerge on all that is our world – where revelation makes some sense of it all – where we can finally see clearly… it's worth it. It really is.

Your word is a lamp to my feet, and a light for my path.

Psalm 119:105 (NRSV)

I recently heard a woman tell her story. She had been pimped and sexually exploited for most of her young teen/adult life. We were training some street outreach volunteers and I had asked my friend (who has been recently set free from that life) if she'd tell her story to help us. One of the questions I asked her was what she thought of volunteers on outreach vans. She explained that she rarely thought anything about anyone at all… She said it like this:

I was so wrapped up in the streets and my own addiction… even if I was looking at you I was blind. I couldn't see anything.

It was a powerful description of a life lived in darkness. So I asked her, "What made the difference? What got through your blindness?" She answered that it was the persistent kindness and grace of people who had the light. One time (after many times) one act of kindness got through. In the end a kick at the darkness really did bleed daylight and my friend finally saw that there was a way out. She took it.

Now she lives a different life and helps others do the same. It's the power of light and the willingness of people to journey through the darkness to let that light emerge. I asked her if she had any advice for us as we tried to help others like her. She said to never give up. Never stop praying. Never stop trying. All of it makes a difference – whether you can see it or not.

Darkness has a debilitating effect on us. It literally stops us in our tracks, paralysing and preventing us from moving forward. What we desperately need in that moment is light, because it is always light that dispels darkness.

Questions

- Is there a situation or context where you feel "stuck" in the chaos and darkness?

- Who around you is having this experience? Why is that?

- In your local community context, what feels like it is in paralysis?

An old friend of mine called John suffers from Parkinson's disease. His body is much more fragile than it used to be, he struggles to walk and his speech is slow and sometimes unclear. I was speaking at an event where we were considering how we can become people who engage in fighting injustice. My friend was in the audience.

At the end of the talk I asked all the people present if they would like to make a response to the things they had heard. As a way of marking this response, I asked them to choose to walk to the front and make their footprint in some sand that was placed along the edge of the platform. Many people started to move from their seats and make their way to the front. My friend John was among them. He was being helped on either side by two other people and he was slowly making his way towards the platform with very faltering steps. But he did make it. Each step he took was deliberate and intentional, and each one a victory over the disease that told his body he could not do it.

As I watched John, I became acutely aware of how easily we are paralysed by the darkness that chaos brings. That can be true for us personally, or in our work context. We may be faced with a mountain so high that the easiest option is to turn back or give up, or worse still, stay exactly where we are! There is a danger that we remain static and therefore paralysed into non-action and make no progress. So we need to learn how to see light piercing the darkness; to be able to spot it and be drawn to it even when those around us remain caught in the darkness. We need a "curtains being pulled back in the morning" moment where light or revelation floods in.

Perhaps we are trying to work out what comes next in the development of a programme or piece of work we are delivering in a chaotic urban community. And what we need (and long for) is the way ahead to be revealed; we need the light to be switched on; we need the path ahead illuminating. We need light to separate us from the darkness.

But revelation or light do not come in the standing still. They are revealed in the doing, in the going. An old prophet said:

> **If you do away with the yoke of oppression, with the pointing finger and malicious talk, and if you spend yourselves on behalf of the hungry and satisfy the needs of the oppressed, then your light will rise in the darkness, and your night will become like the noonday.**
>
> Isaiah 58:9–10 (NIV)

Going camping in the open countryside is a brilliant way to reconnect with nature. And when you look up on a clear night, all you see are stars. Look around you and all is dark and formless without definition. Look up and there is light. And over time your eyes begin to grow used to the darkness and the seemingly distant light of the stars somehow reaches into the gloom around you. Things that had no clarity start to take on shape and distinction. You cannot hurry the darkness away, but it gradually diminishes because light comes.

As a small child I got lost in the middle of a busy city. I think I misplaced my parents for about three minutes, but in my childlike mind I had lost them and therefore I was lost too. So I stood like a statue in the middle of a main shopping street surrounded by people who were all bigger, taller and louder than me and started looking very carefully for something or someone I might recognize. I looked at clothing and faces. I listened for voices and laughter. And most importantly, I listened for someone who was calling my name. As I stood there, with tears welling up in my eyes fearing I was lost for ever, surrounded by chaos and confusion, I heard my mum. She was calling my name and she was doing our "family whistle". Through all the people I could hear her and I recognized her and I began very carefully to move towards her voice and her whistle.

We have to have the courage to stop momentarily and listen and look to where the light is coming from. It may take a while to spot it but it will come. And when it does we must take ourselves, those we lead and the communities we are working with towards that light.

Taken from *The Lord of the Rings: The Two Towers* by J. R. R. Tolkien:

> Sam: "I know. It's all wrong. By right we shouldn't even be here. But we are. It's like in the great stories, Mr. Frodo. The ones that really mattered. Full of darkness and danger, they were. And sometimes you didn't want to know the end. Because how could the end be happy? How could the world go back to the way it was when so much bad had happened? But in the end, it's only a passing thing, this shadow. Even

darkness must pass. A new day will come. And
when the sun shines it will shine out the clearer."

Dawn does break. Light does come. Whatever situation we
are in personally or whatever we are faced with as a leader of
people, it is our task to seek out that light: divine light. That
means asking for help and waiting patiently, knowing it isn't
something that can be hurried.

Back in the Sinai desert, the dawn came gradually. It didn't
appear all at once; it emerged beautifully in incredible
colour. The divine was in the midst of it. And as the sun got
higher the light flooded the landscape, illuminating hills
and mountains. The torch that we had used to climb the
mountain was nothing in comparison to this light.

Questions

- Where are you in need of the light to overcome darkness?

- Are you looking in the right places for the light to come?

- Is there anything you want to give up on at the moment? Why is this?

- Do you have a tendency to see the mountain climb simply as a problem, rather than to engage fully in the experience of the journey and the perspective possible on reaching your destination?

- Do you feel lost at this moment in the work and/or the people you are leading? Why is this? What is missing? What do you need to change?

- How do you feel about persevering and waiting for the light to come?

- When you are tempted to give up, how do you resist? What might help you to do this even more effectively? Whose help do you need to ask for?

- What is the story that you are holding on to as you wait for the light to come and the darkness to fade?

- What is the greatest challenge you are facing at the moment?

Chapter Four

Think Bigger

After chaos came light. After light came the separation of sea and sky – the formation of expanse. Expanse is one of those "edgeless" words; it is about a wide, open space. This can be a difficult concept for us to connect with. We don't often spend time in wide, open spaces and so our experience of expanse is, ironically, restricted. More and more people are choosing to live in urban contexts surrounded by buildings and people and a skyline that is defined by its human-made origins. People literally see only as far as their gaze allows them – which is probably what is directly in front of their faces. And they live and have vision only for that space, not seeing beyond or around it. In that way people become alienated from a bigger and broader view of life, becoming satisfied with living in a small story with a limited perspective and reduced vision.

On occasion we experience something which reminds us of a much bigger picture and an increased sense of space and expanse. A good friend and I took a road trip recently in the Canadian Rockies. It is a little tricky to explain just how immense the expanse of the landscape is. The roads stretch for miles and whichever way you look you are surrounded by the most breathtaking mountains. And just when you think there can't be more you turn a corner in the road and there, right in front of you, is even more to take your breath away.

My friend and I stayed pretty quiet during some of those moments, just breaking the silence on occasion to simply say "Wow!" or to comment on the incredible beauty of God's creation. Our quietness, which for us was a miracle in itself, probably spoke more than words about how we were being impacted by what was happening in and through nature right before our eyes. I think we were feeling slightly overwhelmed by the scale of the land mass and the height of the mountains and the way they touched the sky. It all seemed so huge and, in comparison, we felt so small and insignificant.

> **I must confess to a feeling of profound humility in the presence of a universe which transcends us at almost every point. I feel like a child who while playing by the seashore has found a few bright coloured shells and a few pebbles while the whole vast ocean of truth stretches out almost untouched and unruffled before my eager fingers.**
>
> Sir Isaac Newton

We often struggle to even enter into the expanse and all that it offers. It is as though we are in our car, approaching the breathtaking landscape, but because of the knocks we have received in life and the pain that we carry we feel unable to lift our eyes to see all that lies ahead of us. We'd rather focus on the radio or the CD player than look up and enjoy the view.

I was part of a venture to bring expanse to some marginalized, broken people in a lower social economic area of Vancouver, Canada. The women of the area (particularly those who are stuck in the oppressive clutches of commercial sexual oppression) are invited every second month to come on a retreat called The Journey. The retreat is held on the beautiful Sunshine Coast of British Columbia. A stunning ride on a ferry transports you there. One thing that has shocked me about the experience has been the amount of women who have lived in Vancouver (which is surrounded by water) their whole lives and have never been on a ferry before. After first noticing this tendency, I met a man who hadn't actually looked up in over a year. He had been bent over looking for crack cocaine on the sidewalks of Vancouver's "hood" for a year!

Those are extreme examples of the smallness that our lives can hold but it has remained a true principle. When we live self-centred and orderly lives they are often characterized by smallness. Consider what the damages of life can do as well.

A friend was working through some challenging issues in her life and was battling hard to live in such a way that she wasn't defined by her past and all of the experiences that had been part of it. As hard as she tried to forget all that had gone before, she just couldn't shake it off. It affected her friendships and her ability to trust anyone. The story of our pasts can very effectively obscure our vision of the future and our awareness of expanse that comes with that.

In the end my friend went and spoke to a vicar. She simply explained that her story included pain and it seemed to chase her. This man of the cloth looked at her, smiled and said that it was just because life is often sh*£! And in that very moment it was as if my friend was able to walk into an open space, the past recognized and underlined and the journey ahead clear and unmapped. Light was certainly followed by expanse. And the minister gave her the words that lifted her gaze and her eyes onto the expanse ahead.

In the process of discovering God's creative power, the movement out of chaos, seeing and breathing in expanse, is vital. But being able to see expanse, to see the big picture and the big story, is not something that happens easily.

A few years ago there was a craze for Magic Eye 3D images. These require a particular skill and ability to work out what is hidden in the pattern presented. You have to look at the image carefully, and almost without warning suddenly what is really present comes into focus. But you have to look at the whole image.

God doesn't normally shed light that leads us to shallow places. The shepherds of the Nativity are great examples of this. They were living small lives, wrapped up in the little drama of their own existence. Angels, accompanied by a symphony of light and revelation, invited them into something eternally more grand and wonderful than their puny lives. They ran to take the invitation and, in running, plunged into a dimension that was perpetually bigger than anything they could have dreamed of. They ran into the depth of the re-creation of the world. A whole new world was emerging from the initial ordering of divine light. Now, they were invited into the expanse of it.

I get a chuckle out of thinking what it must be like for the shepherds to realize that they are represented every year in the telling of the most glorious story on earth every Christmas. You can't have the story of the incarnation retold without the shepherds. That's because Divine Order introduced chaos, brought revelation and then expanded the lives of ordinary, run-of-the-mill shepherds and made them soar to new heights of discovery and salvation.

The reality is that sometimes the weight or the circumstances we are in, or the seemingly unending pursuit of justice for those unable to speak for themselves, or the reoccurring exhaustion of leading an organization all have a way of causing us to lose our sense of expanse. Expanse can seem incredibly scary when you are feeling overwhelmed. The danger of losing this large view is that it really is our ultimate connection, our root to why we do what we do. Without this anchor we can be set adrift of our motivation and purpose.

To consider...

• What is your answer to the "why" of your life?

• Why do you do the job you do?

• Why do you live where you live?

• When you get out of bed in the morning, how do you approach your day?

• What would you like to change about your life if you had the chance?

• What would you like to change about your work situation?

• What is the one thing you would like to change about the community you are part of?

When we are in the process of launching a new piece of work in our local communities, we can lose sight of the big story and the big picture (as can those we journey with). The same is true when we are in the middle of personal struggle and chaos. And also in a group setting.

Walk around any city and very rarely will you see people looking upwards. Instead you look straight ahead. Anthony Gormley placed a series of statues in the vicinity of the Thames in London around the areas known as Southbank and the Embankment. Some of these statues were placed at eye level. Tourists enjoyed having their photos taken with them. You could touch them. They were a little larger than lifesize so it was always a surprise to meet one on the pavement! But I think very few people noticed the ones that had been placed on top of the roofs of a number of buildings in the area. They were high up, beyond the immediate line of sight. They looked down on everyone, literally from a great height. They were placed to be able to see the expanse of London and not to get caught in the middle of the small.

Expanse is found from a different perspective.

In my own life I've had times where I began to question if what I did truly mattered. Because of circumstances I had lost sight of why I chose to live the way I do. I remember complaining to a friend who suggested I write my ideal job description out and pray about it. I thought it was a great idea. So I began to write a list of things I would do if nothing was in my way – to live what I believed and felt called to. As the list began to form I started to see something. The list I had created was the list I was living (with a few exceptions). I was actually living in the expanse but I had lost sight of it – a "can't see the forest for the trees" kind of situation. This can happen more often than we think. Much of the time we need to spend with God is about Him reminding us of the bigger story we are in. The meaning of what we do. Why it matters. How it fits.

One of the characteristic marks of recent times has been the absence of a grand narrative, a big story or a big picture in which people can place their lives and understand their purpose. Postmodernism has brought much creativity and freedom to people, and that freedom has afforded them the space and opportunity to ask questions in a way they have not been able to before. But without the existence of an ultimate truth, people have been left wanting.

Now here is my secret – I tell it to you with an openness of heart that I doubt I shall ever achieve again, so I pray that you are in a quiet room as you hear these words. My secret is that I need God – that I am sick and can no longer make it alone. I need God to help me to give, because I no longer seem capable of giving; to

> help me be kind, as I no longer seem capable
> of kindness; to help me love, as I seem beyond
> being able to love ...[6]

For many people, the experience of expanse can be daunting and even scary. It can feel like the "unknown", and because of that it feels an unsafe and potentially insecure place to be. But it is for this reason that you need to return to the big story; the underpinning vision and reason for what you do, why you do it and how you do it. Imagine undertaking a journey with no sense of destination or goals. Without those things you are probably already lost! Without this sense of big story/big picture backdrop, times can become very tough. We simply roll around between all the immediate things that face us rather than dealing with them in the light of the long-term vision that guides us.

This is a deep spiritual truth. Even our relationship with God can be smaller than it needs to be. When we try to structure God and the way He works, we actually miss out on the mysterious adventure that He has for us – an adventure that is designed not to make life more predictable, but to strengthen our faith in a God whose ways are much higher than our ways.

I remember when I was starting to experiment with prayer exercises designed to help us imagine and have conversations with God. I was using my imagination to envision a safe place where I could have a talk with Jesus. I imagined myself on a bench overlooking the ocean (a real place on an old running route of mine). I would sit down on the bench and Jesus would appear dressed like the *Mission Impossible* man. He would be in a trench coat with a hat and the music would start playing and He would hand me a note (my mission, should I choose to accept it).

It was a bit dramatic and funny at the same time. Every time I would do this prayer-visioning exercise it would be the same vision. Eventually I was intrigued and so when Jesus showed up I just asked Him, "Why do we keep meeting like this?" Jesus responded by saying, "I thought you'd never ask!" and took off His "costume" and sat down beside me like a friend. He had a lot more things to show me about His character and the nature of our relationship. He is much more than a mission-giver. He is a lover, friend, leader, teacher, partner, and much, much more than that. The invitation God gives us is to a relationship that is constantly expanding. As soon as our relationship with Him becomes stagnant and small – as soon as God Himself becomes controllable – we have lost the essence of what it means to be spiritual. We've lost a true vision of a living God.

This is true in every relationship. In the absence of a guiding overarching vision, tensions between co-workers can come to the surface. Teams need a cause and a focus for their work. They need to know what they are contributing to as they carry out their role. When this isn't present, or dims in people's minds, those things that would normally just be lived through become things that break teams, and the work they do, apart. Initial agreement over shared vision becomes like glue uniting those involved, despite any existing tensions. But over time this initial agreement can fade.

A phone call with a colleague was a strong reminder of this. My colleague, and friend, explained that she was feeling as though she didn't know what she was a part of and how the work she was doing contributed to the bigger picture. She had lost sight of the vision she had originally bought into. She had changed cities and moved into a community that was characterized by a number of challenging social issues. She was 150 miles from her nearest family. And right now, things were tough and relationships were tense. As a leader I had three immediate tasks:

- Listen carefully and actively to what was being said.

- Encourage my colleague, thanking her for the sacrifices she had made and the incredible beginnings of community development that were now taking place.

- Retell the story that she had initially aligned herself with and ask her to place herself within that.

The role of a leader is to tell this big story once and then tell it a thousand more times. And on the route through, encourage those following that they are playing their part in bringing the ultimate vision to completion.

One writer in the Bible explained, "Where there is no vision, the people perish".[7]

Expressing expanse, painting the picture is essential. This isn't only true in the context of growing in leadership. It is also true with regard to our own personal growth and development. Muhammad Yunus was awarded the Nobel Prize for his pioneering method of banking which combats poverty by the development of micro-finance projects with some of Asia's poorest people. When asked what motivated his work, his response was powerful and yet very simple. He explained that he imagined a world in which poverty did not exist. He went on to say, "You can only build what you can imagine." Yunus sees expanse and has trodden confidently into it. But his steps have been firmly guided by an underpinning vision.

Questions

- What do you enjoy most about life?

- What would your life motto be?

- How often do you remember this or think about it?

- What are the things that obscure or mar your vision?

- Do you have a sense of being "called" in life?

- How does this affect the choices you make?

- Chart the big choices you have made in the past five years. What are the things that determined those choices? What pattern do you notice?

- What are you doing at the moment to help you see the whole picture?

- What are your reasons for doing what you do?

- What are the things that block your vision of the big picture?

- What do you need to do differently as a result of the way you have answered these questions?

Chapter Five

Holding the Landing

> The whole difference between construction and
> creation is exactly this: that a thing constructed
> can only be loved after it is constructed; but a
> thing created is loved before it exists.
>
> Charles Dickens

Many years ago I went skydiving. A friend and I endured the "lessons", were certified in a few hours and then got in a little plane, ascended to the right height and jumped out.

It's against every normal instinct in your body to jump out of a moving plane. We had practised in a barn – jumping from the top level and learning to land with all our parachute gear on. But nothing really prepares you for the actual reality of throwing yourself out, many thousands of feet in the air, while the earth below shoots by you and the air is too cold to breathe – if you are still breathing, that is. I loved it. I love adventure and crazy things. I love getting my heart pumping and so I enjoyed the journey of the jump. I loved the "throw yourself out of a plane" bit and then the parachute opening automatically (on your first jump) and I loved the soaring through the wide open spaces – floating in the air and enjoying the view. I even managed to use the controls to steer. It was great fun.

The hardest part of jumping is the landing. Funny. You wouldn't think that but it's true. As much as the jumping is a white-knuckle affair, the landing is trickier. You have the earth rushing up towards you – you are descending at a decent clip – you've got to bend your knees and brace yourself for impact and at the same time you've got to tuck and roll so you don't break your ankles or leg bones. You've got to pay attention but not look down – if you look down you panic and you instinctively lock up and break your leg. You've got to keep your eye on the horizon and resist the urge to look at the earth quickly approaching underneath you, and then you've got to keep some momentum… so land light, tuck and roll.

The landing. That's almost always the tricky bit if you think about it.

It's hard to get the landing right. I remember watching Olympic gymnastics with my mother… no matter how high the women jumped or how great the routine was, we all waited for the landing. The landing generates the majority of the points. If the gymnast can't "land" then the routine is just standard. If the routine is amazing and the landing solid, the chances of a win are good. I actually remember holding my breath for the landing. *Can the gymnast hold the landing?*

In a beautiful messy Kingdom life we embrace the chaos. A bit like jumping out of a moving plane. We see the light of what is possible – of the hope and life that come from the Source. Our lives begin to get bigger. We are led to wide-open spaces... room to dream and live and be. Room to expand our horizon – see the bigness of the plan. And then we land. The landing can be the hardest bit. Finding our footing on a sure foundation is the way forward.

Landing well is essential to creating a foundation that will enable us to sustain new life. Without a place to "stand" we are easily blown by whatever wind comes our way. The forces of life blow hard and the pressures seem to increase over time... Without a rootedness we can topple. We can be lost in the re-creation process if we don't allow God to help us "land" on a solid foundation.

When God creates and fashions the earth, the landing is also key; it's the part where things are made real and tangible and solid. It's the foundation out of which all the rest of life will grow. It's the basis of our food, water source, the reciprocal relationship between plants and the earth. And it's the same in our Kingdom life.

Landing is key.

God wants to help us land by creating a foundation in each of us. A place where we can be established. Where our "new life" can take root and grow deep, so it isn't a fickle thing that can be easily destroyed. This new life is intended to last. We want to live lives that are dug down deep. Don't worry, though; if you think this sounds like having a rootedness that will mean the same as being stuck or small – it won't be. The kind of land God wants to create involves movement.

In the Genesis story, the landing is not a foundation like that of a concrete house – it is a spacious expanse. Land, with plants, vegetation and fruit. The image of the first creation is that the establishment of land was organic in origin. Instead of concrete, it was a living organism that grew and bore fruit. The image is that even the foundation is alive – not static and predictable, but wild, free, and alive with life.

The foundation is a breathing body, not a stagnant base.

Like your life.

The landing is essential but it's not the end… It's the beginning, the foundation from which everything else grows. If you get the landing right, you will last through thick and thin.

Psalm 1 compares our lives of righteousness (when we live with God's order) with this original ordering of creation. "That person is like a tree planted by streams of water, which yields its fruit in season and whose leaf does not wither – whatever they do prospers".[8] To be rooted is to be established. It means to be secure but also alive. Growing fruit – always emerging with newness of life renewed. Jesus said, "I have come that [you] may have life, and have it to the full".[9] What could be fuller than a consistently growing and reproducing garden?

But to get the landing right requires time and work. The soil is rich and deep. To really grow a solid foundation takes some investment. Think about the story Jesus told about the builder who built his house on the sand. It was easier to build, it required a lot less work – and as soon as a storm came it was blown away. How many of us have built our lives on foundations like that? Sometimes we have the best routine – our lives are like world-class gymnasts; we twist and jump and are beautiful to behold – but we just can't hold the landing. We can't stand when we really need too. We live spectacularly flimsy lives. When a storm comes, our marriage turns out to be shallow, our friends turn out to be fickle, and our lives lack the established place to land.

I sat next to a guy on a plane one time. I had missed my first flight and this was the next one I could find. It required a lot of embracing chaos to carry on… but I did. When I sat down I discovered that the guy next to me was just visiting the city and had flown there a few days before. He said he had sat next to an "evangelist" on his first flight. Then he asked me, "What do you do?" With a completely straight face I said, "I'm an evangelist." I watched him turn pale.

I broke the awkward silence by asking him straight up, "How long have you been running from God?" He looked shocked. "How did you know?" This isn't rocket science. Two travelling evangelists on two flights over a weekend? Are you kidding me?

He began to tell me his story. It was about a life without any foundation. There was nothing strong enough to earth him in realness. Nothing deep enough to keep him strong and healthy when the seasons changed. It was shallow and sad. Money, sex, shallow relationships, climbing a corporate ladder that collapsed, the show of success without the depth of it.

He hadn't held the landing. His life was built on the wrong stuff.

We talked for the whole flight. He poured out his heart and I listened. He asked what he could do to change it all. I mentioned I knew Someone who let people start again. The whole process often began with chaos and messy brokenness, but God was waiting in the midst of it to bring some order. There was a way to begin again with Jesus. Jesus could offer a new way to live. Forgiveness, healing, hope, light, future, and foundation. All of it rooted and established so it wouldn't just be blown away.

He could land with Jesus.

He wanted to. He decided to. He couldn't wait too. He needed to grow a life that had some depth to it. So we prayed. When we were collecting our bags he came over to thank me. He said, "You saved my life tonight." I thought that was a nice thing to say, but I reminded him that only Jesus had the ability to save people and give them a brand new start. "Oh no, that's not what I meant," he said. "I had planned it all out. I was going to end everything tonight. Now, I want to live."

The landing is key. Depth, earthiness, rootedness. In a culture obsessed with shallow living and shiny, easy success, rootedness cannot be bought or assumed; it has to be grown. It is a process. That's why God uses the gardening image so much in the Bible. And why He kicks off creation with a living earth instead of a *lifeless* building.

In Matthew 13:32, Jesus compares faith to the seed that would be planted in the ground: "Though it is the smallest of all seeds, yet when it grows, it is the largest of garden plants and becomes a tree, so that the birds come and perch in its branches" (NIV). Jesus goes on to compare our hearts to the ground on which the seed falls (Mark 4). The idea is that just as creation was developed with the foundation of land (garden), so is the re-creation of our lives.

Rootedness. Planting. Gardens. Earth. Land. It's all connected in us. We are made of dirt – that's how God tells the story. And we all return to the dirt. But in the meantime, how we live matters. Our connections, our desires, our relationships need to be tended to like a garden. Rooted and established in good soil. We need things in our lives that matter. Things that are beyond function and hold truth that is eternal. We need a depth of being that will endure past the hard times and into the future. We need a hope that is secure.

I know a married couple who are amazing. They are deep and lovely and the love they have for each other is tangible. It's not new – it's seasoned. It's beautiful. I asked one of them once how it happened that they love each other so deeply. She told me of the tragic death of their youngest son. He was killed by a car and they went through the trauma together. There are many who believe that there is an extremely high divorce rate (80 to 90 per cent) when a couple loses a child. Those claims are based on statistics from a study done by Teresa Rando in 1985.[10] Most couples who go though the loss of a child don't last. They knew this. And at the hospital, over the deathbed of their youngest son, they prayed together. They asked God to somehow take the brokenness of their son's death and use it to build them together. It was foundational. Their relationship is not accidentally deep. It is deep by design. It is rooted and established in the reality of pain and tragedy, but in the promise that God can keep us. God can sustain us. God can deepen us. They landed. And it's a beautifully, deep, foundational landing.

Revelation. Expanse. Land. The seed is the truth, the land is our hearts and we need to allow the work of building the right foundations in our lives to begin here. The fruit of it all is re-creation. We become the well-watered garden of God-sized proportions. Good land bears fruit. This is a central part of God's plan for us. It is never static.

So the invitation is to land. To hold the landing. To embrace this Kingdom life with tenacity and intention. To dig deep with God as He leads us to foundational truths that will root and establish us in Him.

Questions

- Do you find it easier to jump than to land? Who can you ask to help you with this?

- What words would others use to describe your life currently?

- Over this past week, what has been the fruit of your life?

- Are you working on your character development at the moment? What are you noticing?

- What pressures are you experiencing? Are your foundations solid enough to sustain you?

- How much time are you investing in building the foundations of your life? Do you need to invest more?

- Is there a sense in which your life is static or stuck, or is it rich with life, movement and growth?

- Where do you sense a need for greater depth in your life?

- Are you running towards or away from God?

- Are you living the kind of life you love?

Chapter Six

Seasons

Life is about movement. After God establishes a foundation of land in the creation account, albeit a growing, moving, breathing groundwork, He moves on to create the seasons. This is in stark contrast to our normal understanding of building. If the seasons do anything at all, they flow with constant change in an already lively universe.

Isn't that amazing? In the order of creation God makes sure that everything changes all the time. Control freaks beware. Everything changes. All the time. Nothing will ever stand still. Nothing will ever stop – everything will be rotating and shifting and moving. Life will always be about movement. It's fascinating, especially considering our capacity to want to be in control. To have everything "ordered" in the fashion of a clock.

The Creation (in German, *Die Schöpfung*) is an oratorio written by the composer Joseph Haydn from 1796–98. The oratorio is about the creation of the world that we've been talking about. The mightiest of the choruses of *The Creation* and a popular favourite is No. 13, "*Die Himmel erzählen die*

Ehre Gottes" ("The heavens are telling the glory of God"). It is the depiction of the creation of the seasons and the words are mostly from Psalm 19:1–3:

The heavens declare the glory of God; the skies proclaim the work of his hands. Day after day they pour forth speech; night after night they reveal knowledge. There is no speech, they use no words; no sound is heard from them. (NIV)

Haydn's century, following Newton's discoveries but preceding those of Darwin, was the heyday of the view that an orderly universe provides clear evidence of divine wisdom. Haydn inherently understood and sought to proclaim through his musical genius that God was not fully "knowable". The sheer and vast beauty of the heavens was enough to "sing" of the otherness of God. The glory of God is connected to His "bigness", evidenced by the immensity of the heavens.

Haydn was more right then he could have known.

Today, scientists tell us that we are unable to even see the "heavens" in their entirety – indeed, we cannot even know the extent of them. It sounds like God. It sounds like the kind of God we can't control or limit or put in a box – because God is bigger than the box. It's like the old joke about the scientist who challenges God to a creative contest. The scientist shows up with a bucket of dirt and God says, "Hey – make your own dirt."

God is so much bigger and larger than we can even comprehend. Sometimes it's important to recall that. The atheist who told me the other day that he didn't believe in God was surprised when I responded, "I'll be sure to let him know." God's existence isn't like the Easter Bunny or Santa Claus. He does not *need* us to believe in Him to exist. We exist because He believes in us. He's bigger than us. And He's trying to communicate with us. Life is movement.

I was just talking to a friend who is due to give birth in a month or so. It's a terrible time as far as pregnancy goes. You are very large and swollen and your energy is at a low. You are tired of waiting… because you've been at this "creation" thing for almost a year already. It's a long haul. You are forced to slow down by this point and it's like time itself starts working backwards. The longer you stare at the clock the slower the time goes. Everyone you talk to (especially other mothers) assure you that this is just a season… and it's going to change fast! But it's hard to believe. And then it happens. The baby comes. And everything changes. Time starts moving in fast forward. Movement is an understatement. It's like a cosmic shifting. The first baby is a massive learning curve – it feels like someone has sped up time and it slips through your fingers as you try to hang on to it. Life is movement.

So why do we struggle with change? God built constant change into the cosmos. He intended for things to have a time, and for time to shift and grow and for the earth to rotate and for the stars to burn out and for the seasons to arise and fall. Constant change. Why are we so afraid?

I think we are afraid of things we can't control. Seasons are something we cannot control. If I could control the seasons I would banish winter. I just survived a very cold one in northern Canada. Just survived. "I want a different season please!" is what I said to God. But I had to wait. It's out of my control. There, I said it. And everything that reminds me of my smallness – of my humanness – I like to push under the rug. I like to push down my own little-ness into the very depth of me and try to forget it. So I control everything I can and focus my attention on those things. I make them look good and attractive and I tell others to look at those things too… but if I'm honest – and on occasion I try to be – I'll admit that there are many more things that I cannot control. God being the first thing. Seasons being another.

Deserts and winters. They are part of the ever-changing landscape of God's great plan for my life. You ever think about that? The Bible says that after Jesus announced His plan to be the one who would save the world, the Spirit led him into the wilderness. While there He was tempted to find a quick route out of that wilderness. But he didn't give in.

The Spirit.

Led Him.

Into.

The wilderness.

And He stayed there until it had served its purpose. Why?

Different seasons have different strengths. They do different things. To the earth, everything has a purpose and a meaning. Even winter has its purposes. The wilderness was a place for Jesus to sort out what kind of a man He was going to be. What sort of a strategy He was going to use to actually do the work He was sent to do.

The winter season of our lives tends to have a similar theme – if we will look for it. Early saints in the church used to call a winter season of the soul the "dark night" and it was a season where people struggled to find God. Today, after reading Mother Teresa's journals, it would seem she was in that season for a long time. Winter. In the heat of the city of Calcutta, as the sidewalk seemed to cook the skin of the poorest of the poor, she would stoop and smile and pick up the homeless and the forgotten and she would see Jesus in them. That's what she said. She saw Jesus in the poor.

She saw Jesus there because she couldn't see Him in her dreams or her visions or her prayers any more. He had disappeared. It was winter in her soul. What kind of a "lover" would she be in the winter? That seemed to be the question she thought God was asking her. How will you serve me if you can't "feel" me? She started to understand as she walked through this winter season that it actually served as a gift to help her to identify with her people. They were forgotten and alone and rejected and, well, in their own personal winter forever. The winter season was teaching her – helping with her prayer to join in the sufferings of Christ. She was learning to live by faith through the very winter season of her soul. She started to thank God for the emptiness. When was the last time you thanked God for an empty feeling inside of you?

The idea of accepting seasons as gifts is an affront to a culture that demands happiness as the one season of our lives. It's a sad reality of our culture that it demands a constant season of "happy". Sad? We've got something for that. Anxious? We've got something else. On and on it goes as we medicate ourselves, if necessary, into a perpetual state of "summer", whether we are in that season or not.

I took my son to a sing-a-long parent session and they were singing the childhood classic, "If you're happy and you know it". When they started to sing the second verse about being angry, I became confused because we never sang the angry bit before. When I was a kid we only sang about one emotion – happiness. And then we made that emotion a lifestyle and an aim. Happiness was the aim of a whole generation. This is in stark contrast to God's Divine Ordering of creation. Wanting only happiness is like being stuck in one season forever. It is limited, ordered, controlled and, frankly, just plain boring.

We do the same with "youth" as we do with "happiness" – controlling ageing through any means necessary. So much money and time spent on these things; yet are we more content or happy or at peace? Why have we forgotten about the beauty and value of wisdom?

Henri Nouwen, a man who loved God and wrote a lot of books about what He is like, crafted a theology (How God works) framed around the circus. He spent a whole year travelling with a circus. He was captivated by the example of the flying trapeze artists. The most appreciated member of the trapeze team, for the audience, is the one who does all the flying and jumping in the air. But the most important member of the trapeze team to the team is the catcher. He's the one you can't see. The trapeze artists are really only free to take the risks they take if they know the catcher is reliable enough to catch them. It's the trust in the catcher that enables them to be truly free. And this is the issue with things we cannot control. If we are willing to risk it and trust God, we can embrace the seasons that come our way.

If we are to take risks, to be free, in the air, in life, we have to know there's a catcher. We have to know that when we come down from it all, we're going to be caught; we're going to be safe. The great hero is the least visible. And most of us are stuck on a ledge, in a season we don't understand, trying to will ourselves, or medicate ourselves, into summer.

This kind of living brings a different perspective – look up, look out, see the vastness. Know that it is beyond your control, but behind its breathtaking vastness is God the

Catcher and the Sustainer through the seasons... and we can trust Him.

God models for us the fully engaged, creative heart that longs for all seasons to deepen our lives and wants to lead us to deeper places, where even winter is a teacher that we can thank God for. The writer of Ecclesiastes understood that there was a time for everything under heaven. The greatness of this beautiful life is that it is not predictable, boring, and unchanging. It is alive with seasons, times, and shifts. It is that kind of living that brings meaning and beauty in the world – and in our lives. Life is movement.

Questions

- Are you noticing that your life is characterized by movement and change at the moment? How is that making you feel?

- What or who do you try to control? Are there things you need to let go of?

- How do you respond when things seem out of control?

- Do you expend a lot of energy trying to put life in order, yet still feel unsatisfied?

- What "season" do you sense you are in currently? What are you learning?

- Do you love and serve God through all seasons or do you "cool off" when life "feels" less good, less like summer?

- What are the temptations you face in your experience of wilderness?

- What changes can you make to help you not just survive but also thrive in times that seem like the coldest winter?

- Are you pursuing happiness rather than wisdom and depth?

- What might be "the deeper places" that God wants to lead you to?

- What can you do today to restore your perspective and embrace the movement and change in your life?

Chapter Seven

Life: Mind-blowing Simplicity

The first animals that God creates are the birds and the fish. Fish are pretty basic. I remember dissecting one when I was twelve and we started to study biology in science. The reason they pick fish is that they are such a uncomplicated organism. Simple.

Birds, on the other hand, are very complex. Their bones are hollow and bodies light. Their capacity for flight is both puzzling and impressive. Scientists took forever to figure out exactly how they fly.

What God creates on the fifth day is both simple and complex. It is simple and complex *at the same time.*

This is the opposite of what we know about things. Our natural and human instinct insists that things increase or develop in systematic fashion. We believe and trust in the "incremental". Onto foundational knowledge is built increasing complexity.

But God's version of life creation is both simple and complex.

At the same time.

Think about it.

Even the simple truth that God loves you is the most complex theological idea. The love of God is so simple that a child can understand it and so complex that it can bring a theologian to tears. Dr Karl Barth was a complex theologian of the twentieth century. He wrote volume after weighty volume on the meaning of life and faith. A reporter once asked Dr Barth if he could summarize what he had said in all those volumes. Dr Barth thought for a moment and then said: "Jesus loves me, this I know, for the Bible tells me so." Simple and complex. At the same time.

I have a friend who survived the Rwandan genocide. I didn't know she was a survivor until we were in a small group and talking about encountering Jesus.

Encountering Jesus is one of these "simple *and* complex" things. There is actually a story in the Bible (one of my favourite ones) where Jesus heals a blind beggar.[11] The religious folk were trying to trap Jesus into saying or being something heretical so they could stop Him (or at least control Him). So when they heard about this guy who had been healed from his blindness, the religious leaders grabbed him and took him in for questioning. And the questions about Jesus come thick and fast – "Who did He say He was?", "Who do you think He is?", "Is He the Messiah?" – it's almost comical because the now ex-blind guy keeps saying the same thing over and over: "I don't know. All I know is that I was blind but now I see."

So they drag his parents in (clearly they were getting a bit desperate now) so that they could confirm that he really was the guy who was blind – and they say the exact same thing. Something like, "I don't know the complex theological answers to your questions… All I know is he was blind but now he can see." And that's enough.

I was healed. Simple. There it is.

And it's also complex, because Jesus is the Messiah. He is the one who will threaten existing religious structures and power bases. He is the one who will overthrow the elite and give way for the poor. He is ushering in the new Kingdom and everything will change.

Complex. You bet.

And simple.

At the same time.

So, back to Rwanda.

The question my small group was answering was "When have you encountered Jesus?" A good question. Everyone's answer was nice but my friend (let's call her Sam) said, "When I was in the forest." That was nice but I was unsure what she meant. So I asked her and she told me that it was when she and forty other kids had run for their lives after seeing their parents murdered in front of them. They ran to the forest and hid. For forty days. She said that every day they were scared and felt so alone. They would pray. And then Jesus would show up. He showed up in the forest. She said because Jesus showed up they knew they were not alone. They weren't afraid any more. She said many of the children could sleep through the night after Jesus had come. Some other people snuck them food that kept them alive.

The response of the group was overwhelming shock and silence. We had no idea our friend had lived through that kind of horror and that kind of wonder. *At the same time.*

I had a hundred questions. I wanted to know everything. Mostly I wanted to know how she went through that kind of event and managed to survive. To live. To go on living. She said it was simple. (Get where I'm going with this?) She said she chose to forgive. And then she could move on. What? I wondered about this and then asked her about it again later. What did she mean? How did she manage to forgive people who hacked her family to death? How could she do something so incredibly hard? She said it was simple. "I listened to Jesus. He said to forgive my enemies. So I did." There it is again. That incredible simple thing.

I know Jesus said to forgive but forgiveness is complex. It's tricky stuff. Or is it? Perhaps encountering Jesus is simple and complex at the same time. Perhaps listening to Him is the same. We "um" and we "ah" and we waste a lot of time thinking about the theological implications of things and wondering how they line up with our current value systems… but what would happen if we took the truth of the gospel as simple? What would happen if we really lived out the good news? What would our lives look like if we forgave freely? Gave generously? Shared what we had with the hungry and the poor? It would look simple. And complex. At the same time.

That's what God's creative ability does. It creates the most simple and complex things together. Mind-blowing simplicity.

I had my friend tell her story on a message series I was doing on forgiveness. It was incredibly powerful. Obviously her story itself was powerful, but the context where she shared it was even more so. See, I asked her to share her story with a group of people who have been terribly wronged. They are the first peoples of Canada and they have suffered systemic injustices that would make you blush. The people in that audience on that day were filled with complex systems of violence and abuse that would make you dizzy even if you tried to figure them out. None of the people in the audience had ever met someone who had suffered more than them.

Until that day. As my friend began to tell her story you could see everyone in the crowd sit up and start listening (which is a rare beauty). When she got to the "I chose to forgive" bit everything went quiet. You could hear the unuttered questions, "Is it possible?", "Is it true?", "Could it be?" and then some possible dreams unuttered as well: "I could move on?", "I could leave the abuse behind me?"

And this is a simple truth with complex realities. We can move on. Forgiveness is a choice. We don't have to be defined by our past. We can encounter God. We can do what He says. It's mind-blowing simplicity. Birds and fish formed together. The way God works is incredibly simple. So simple, it's complex.

There are several words for life in the Bible. The most basic Greek words are *bios* and *zoe*. *Bios* is obvious... it's our bodies. It's the stuff that we are made of. It's where we get the word "biology". But *zoe* is a Greek word that hints at an incredible truth – it means the essence of life. Our spirit or sense of self. It's the thing Jesus talked about when He said that we were created to have life and have it abundantly. We were created for *bios* and for *zoe*. Life.

And life takes up space. You remember the expanse that made everything bigger... What's the large space for? It's for life. It's to fill.

This is what God is doing on this day of creation. He is filling the space. He uses *all* of what He creates. Life takes up space.

Not just filler but *life* to take up space.

Years ago, our inner-city community partnered with a church in the suburbs. They were great Christian people who genuinely struggled with how to simply obey God and what He commanded while they had empty rooms in their houses. We were part of a community of people trying to make our home among an addicted inner city.

They wondered if they should come and help us with food trucks and sandwiches... We wondered if there wasn't something more, something deeper.

At that time, as we were wondering together about how to partner effectively, we came across a study. The study showed that 90 per cent of the people we were working with, who were adult drug addicts, were from the foster care system. They had no families. They had simply reached the maximum age or run away from foster care and wandered to our section of the city. We realized that what we needed were great families with extra room in their houses. We needed to stop the flow of unwanted kids growing up to be drug addicts. We needed to stop the systemic injustice by providing good foster homes for kids who needed families. But what family that has everything under control, and is established, wants to take the messy risk of fostering kids with special needs?

And then we started to see a creation emerge. We started to understand that maybe all the space in the suburbs, and in the homes with spare bedrooms, and the minivans with extra seats – maybe all that space was *for* something? Maybe those people with stirred hearts for justice could partner in a way that wasn't distant and aloof – maybe they held the solution to a complex social problem – and maybe that solution was actually quite simple.

God fills the space with life. All of it.

Henri Nouwen understood this kind of complexity and simplicity in his own life. He left the halls of academia to embrace a relationship some would categorize as "simple" and the community that they were a part of, L'Arche. (In case you don't know, Henri Nouwen was a professor, lectured at Ivy League schools, authored many books and spoke around the world... climbing the upward ladder of fame and importance. Along the journey he met Jean Vanier and was introduced to the L'Arche communities, who intentionally care for people with extreme physical and mental disabilities. Nouwen came to join this community and leave his successful "career" to simply care for another person. It was a powerful demonstration of countercultural living and impacted a generation.) Nouwen began to understand through this relationship that true life, deep life, is both complex and simple at the same time. Graduate schools such as Yale and Harvard taught him some important things, but a community of "misfits" was a learning ground that filled some of the deep places in him with simplicity and beauty.

Henri Nouwen made a journey to India to explore with Mother Teresa the clue to faithful living. If anyone would know, it was her. Faced with such a profound question, her answer shocks with its simplicity: "Spend an hour with God each day and don't do anything you know is wrong."

Mother Teresa's rule of living was to never refuse Jesus anything. To always let her life be a big "yes" to God. How's that for simple? Now, try living it. Trust me – it gets more complex.

Questions

- Where are you experiencing and noticing the simple and the complex in your life?

- Do you find it difficult to embrace the simplicity of what it means to follow Jesus? Why do you think that is? How would your life be different if you took Jesus at His word?

- How do you respond to the complexity and simplicity of the story of forgiveness described in this chapter? Why is that? Who do you need to forgive?

- What do you need to move on from? Is there anything from your past that is defining your present?

- What or who is helping you understand that deep life is both complex and simple at the same time?

- Do you currently live your life as a big "yes" to God?

- Mother Teresa said, "Spend an hour with God each day and don't do anything you know is wrong." What do you need to change for this to be true in your own life?

Chapter Eight

Humanity

Independence? That's middle-class blasphemy. We are all dependent on one another, every soul of us on earth.

George Bernard Shaw

The creation story in Genesis is actually a poem. And it comes to its climax at the creation of humanity. The creation of humanity is also where this poem deviates from a similar Babylonian creation myth. See, the other creation poem (the Babylonian one) was the dominant cultural view at the time (when this was written, the Israelites were in captivity in Babylon). The Babylonian myth's climax was when God made the king in his own image, to rule over every other person. In other words, the king was the image of God and everyone else was his slave. It kind of stands to reason that an empire built on control and fear had that sort of creation myth. That way, everyone's obedience was fuelled by belief in the godlike nature of their king. And it meant that ordinary people held the belief that they were anything but godlike!

The creation story we read about in the book of Genesis "appears" to have a similar feel – a similar beginning, there are even some phrases that are almost identical, but it has a radically different ending. In the Hebrew poem the created order peaks at the creation of humanity – "... in the image of God he created them; male and female he created them"[12] – and it was very good. Do you notice the difference? We. All of us. Created in God's image. Not just one person. Not just the king. And to top it all, we read and can understand that it was *very good*. You can almost sense God's delight and pleasure.

The implications of this story are incredible. Actually, to be honest, I think we might never fully understand all the implications of this beginning – the depth and meaning of the poem should leave us speechless. Think about it. This was written in a world where no one had any rights. This was before the idea of a human rights charter. This was in barbaric countries. Think Mad Max but in the past instead of the future. This was in tribal warfare. *This was written by slaves.*

This was a poem written when they needed to dig deep to try to make sense of the world they were living in. They went as deep as they could go. They went to the heart of not just who created them, but how and why they were created.

This story truly is the beginning of every story. It gets right to the heart of the matter. It describes a beginning when our value is not in what we do or what status society has given us or taken from us – but what God's original purpose was in creating us. It also gets to the nature of God.

I recently read Malala's story.[13] A young girl shot by the Taliban for speaking out for girls to have the right to go to school, Malala was born in Pakistan, in a society that values boys. In her cultural tradition, when a girl is born it is not a celebration, more of a gathering. Families come and they have a sort of welcome – but it's not like when a boy is born. When a boy is born there is a proper celebration that includes throwing money into the crib as a sign of blessing. When Malala was born, her father declared her a blessing and made his family throw money into her crib. He defied society's norm of gender bias and declared Malala to be beautiful and wanted. To be special. And she was.

In her biography she speaks of her father's treatment as the essential ingredient that gave her the courage and strength to stand up for justice. See, regardless of what society told Malala, no matter how much propaganda the Taliban used to shut her up, Malala knew something that could never be taken away. She knew her value. She was beautiful from the inside out. She was loved. She was born and it was very good.

This beginning can't be more important.

That's what the Hebrew slaves were getting at. It doesn't matter what Babylon says. It doesn't matter how much they treat you like slaves. You were created in the image of God.

You were born to be free. You were born – and you are very good.

I went to visit an incredible woman, Jackie Pullinger, who moved to Hong Kong over forty years ago to minister to drug addicts who were "incurable" and left for garbage in an unpoliced area called the "Walled City". Somehow, through a mixture of her obedience and God's grace, drug addicts would miraculously be delivered as she prayed for them. Years and years of faithfulness and re-creating happened and today there is no more Walled City… the government finally tore it down and gave her and her community over an acre of land to continue their work.

I went to see what she was doing because I worked with drug addicts and didn't have the same kind of success. I wondered what the secret was. She told me something that has changed the way I view my ministry. She told me that what she really did was "re-parent" people. She said that everyone she met who was chronically addicted was unwanted. They were rejected, often even as babies. What she did was welcome them – as they are. She declared them beautiful and valuable. She declared them "very good" and welcomed them into community. And that posture, that truth, changed *everything*. Something shifted inside of them.

It's the same ingredient that made Malala the courageous young woman she is today. It's the same stuff that the Hebrews needed to see through their slavery and into their potential freedom. It's the same thing you and I need to be who we were created to be. It's value. It's knowing who we are. It is back to basics.

It's the original recipe for greatness. We were created not because of some narcissistic god who wanted slaves, or needed company. We were created by a life-giving God who loved us before we were even born. And when we were born, we were the climax of His creation. We were His song. His triumph. His love. We were the ones who were going to reflect Him to the whole world. We know this because He didn't just create us for ourselves. He gave us the greatest gift ever given – the ability to co-create. Making beautiful things. Art, kindness, justice, hope, life itself. He gave us creation possibilities.

See, God creates us, humanity, as a community. But not just any community. A community that is made in His image. We are made to reflect divinity in the world. Not only that, but God assigns us as stewards of the earth. That means, of course, that it's up to us to keep everything a beautiful mess. To manage and care for the earth in all its chaos and beauty. All that space should be filled with life.

Yet something goes terribly wrong. We know this because the entire world seems to be suffering from the results of a deep brokenness that is difficult to explain.

Adam and Eve's decision to try to be their own god and adopt fig leaves as their fashion statement was a bigger than big decision, the consequences of which have impacted all of humanity.

God's design and plan for humanity's stewardship of creation was described in Genesis 2:15, to "take care of it" (NIV). This Hebrew word is *samar*: to keep, guard, to preserve, protect, to watch.

Contrast this with the consequences of the selfish tragedy of humanity's decision to "hide from God" in the relationship between Adam and Eve. Genesis 3:16 says, "Your desire will be for your husband, and he will *rule* over you" (NIV, my italics). The word "rule" is a Hebrew word, *masal*: to rule, govern, control; dominion, not domination. It seems we were created to take care of creation… so how is it that we end up dominating and controlling everything and even one another? What a contrasting picture.

Our calling is a shared "keeping", a birthing of order from community. The results of our disobedience are domination, power, and essentially a new idea in humanity's creation – hierarchy. The unfolding consequences of human independence continued to rip people apart from their communal nature, replacing community with empty loneliness.

Sin didn't just affect the created order – it infected the essence of community from which creation sprang. Its very source was soiled.

We hear it echo in the antithesis of community just one generation later, as Cain, after slaying his own brother, attempts to justify himself before God, saying, "Am I my brother's keeper?"[14] This is a famous saying that people use out of context. Right after Cain asks this question (which is when God asks him where his brother is – which is after Cain has killed his brother in a fit of jealous rage), God answers Cain with a long version of "Well, *yes* – you are."

That's how we were made – together. With value and responsibility for each other. How would that reality change life on this planet? If we all recognized that every one of us were created for everyone else and that we all had value from the inside out?

Well, God seems to be asking the same question throughout history and has been consistent in His desire to keep trying… eventually a re-creation happens. It started with the announcement of a child. Perhaps He started at the bottom of all hierarchical systems to remind us of the value of just being born? Jesus arrives and begins to model what it means to be truly human. After modelling a life like none other, Jesus prays for His disciples as they are sent to take the good news of the re-creation to the whole earth. And then a new community is born. The church. The followers of Jesus. The ones who have understood the first creation story as the deep truth of our re-creation story.

Our lives were chaos. We saw the light that gave us the ability to navigate our way through some pretty dark places. We crawled towards it. Our lives became bigger – we finally had some space to grow and room to breathe. We found a place to stand. We got rooted and established in deep places. We had a sure footing. We grew through seasons of our soul, each turn reflecting deeper truths and greater fruit. Simple and complex at the same time. And then we were invited into the fullness of this beautiful mess – the culmination of new chaos for a re-creating to begin again. Life. To fill the space. To be part of the creation of new things. Beautiful things. Life with value. Filling the space. Ushering in the new creation.

Questions

- What cultural messages about your identity play loudest for you?

- Do you know and believe that you are made in the image of God and are "very good"? How is that affecting your sense of self-worth and purpose?

- How could knowing the truth of being made with purpose, intent and significance affect the people in your community?

- Do you really live as if you were "born to be free"? What would be different if you did?

- Do you recognize *all* people to be of equal value? Is there someone or some people you struggle to see in this way? Why is that?

- What resources are you responsible for? Are you stewarding them well? Are you using them to bring life to others?

- In what ways is your life characterized by creative purpose?

Chapter Nine

Rest: In Defiance of Slavery

The Bible tells us that all of creation is groaning for restoration.[15] I'm groaning with it and I'm not alone. We have become a culture of work. Our frenzy to work harder is most likely tied to the misconception that our work defines us. How many times have you met someone for the first time and asked the question "So, what do you do?" to which the reply is, 99.9 per cent of the time, a summary of the job they do, the stuff they get paid for according to the hours they put in. Fascinating. We never list the things we do out of love, or our relationships. Or the things that bring us joy, fullness, and meaning. Some of us, if we are extremely blessed, have the capacity to love what we do as a job – but that still doesn't define us.

Ralph Neighbour, in a new believer's discipleship manual entitled the *The Arrival Kit*,[16] says that we have been wired the wrong way by the world for our whole lives. We have been taught that our happiness and value come from outside of us. You don't have to look far or long to validate that claim... every advertisement is a blatant suggestion that happiness can be bought. Your boyfriend gives you status. Your looks make you happy. Your shape defines your treatment from others. Your job status makes you important.

In the kingdom of God, we start to understand that our value is intrinsic. It comes from inside of us. It is a part of who we are. God loved us before we could ever "do" anything to please Him. We cannot lose the favour of God – we can only reject it.

This reality changes everything. I think this idea alone is part of the incredible revelation of God's Kingdom and how He re-creates us. We cannot be defined by what we do. We are more than that. We were not created to "work"; we were created to be fruitful, creative and filled with life. And part of all that is rest.

You know who never gets to rest? Slaves. Slaves can never rest because they have slave drivers and serve at their mercy. You know who were slaves? The people of God. They were enslaved when they wrote that creation story we talked about earlier. They understood the gift of rest. They knew they wanted it and needed it. They sensed the freedom of it. It's only a free man who can rest. But people trying to survive can never take a break. They are enslaved.

We run a retreat for women who are sexually exploited on the street. For many of them, it's their first ever proper rest. The kind of rest where you never have to worry about someone attacking you in your sleep. The kind of rest that you won't have to pay for later. The kind of rest where your whole body, mind and spirit can just be. Jesus talks about this and I think about it every time I invite a woman to this retreat. "Come to me, all you who are weary and burdened, and I will give you rest".[17] It's such a beautiful invitation. Especially when you know how people live.

So many people, maybe you, live without quality rest in the rhythm of their lives.

A few years back I went on a homeless project and stayed out on the street with some friends as homeless people for several days. One of the things we noticed more than anything else was the lack of rest.

We were moved on by police.

We were awoken in the middle of the night by teenagers partying it up and making fun of us.

No rest.

And we had nowhere warm or soft to sleep so it was hard to fall asleep at all.

Still no rest.

After two days we had almost lost our minds. We were delirious and unable to function properly. Not necessarily because of our poverty – but because we couldn't rest.

This is exactly the condition of humanity when we don't take God up on His offer – when we refuse to recognize the important creative process of rest to our bodies, minds and spirits.

It is no mistake that I'm writing this section now. My energy, mind, and ability to write had been sapped by an insane schedule of duties and responsibilities until my brain was mush. A good friend of mine offered to take me on a trip for a week – just a rest.

I slept in, spent time in the sun, frolicked, and simply wasted time. I didn't check my emails once, didn't call anyone, didn't need to "do" anything. It was the most relaxing time I've had in a long time. Usually, I manage to slip a holiday into a "work" occasion, but not this time. I'm on the plane now, reviewing my notes and realizing that rest is often the missing ingredient in most people's lives.

In my life I often feel guilty for resting. Perhaps it's my great Protestant work-ethic upbringing – or perhaps lurking somewhere within me is the sneaky suspicion that my value is determined by my success. I'm not sure of the exact reason. Choosing to rest feels like an awkward and uncomfortable choice, though, for many of us. And it seems after reading some stories in the Bible that the same was true for some of the characters there as well.

All I know is that rest didn't "come upon" anyone in the Bible either.

Instead, they entered rest on purpose.

It was a choice that they made.

They rested in obedience to God's design.

And they chose to rest when they were free – as a sign

of their freedom and as a defiance of slavery. They were no longer enslaved externally by whips and schedules of the oppressor. And they were no longer slaves internally, by a desire to work themselves into some kind of valuable commodity. They were made in the image of God, and God rested and so did they. They entered rest *by believing* God.

Rest might be more of a faith issue than a time constraint.

In order to rest you have to trust that God can take care of the world, even your world. Some things can wait for God's time. You have to simply believe that God is God, not you. Resting was a part of the created order because everything needs a rest – including people.

It's also a test of our ability to trust God with provision. Resting from work means less work which means less money. If money is our god we are enslaved to work. It's that simple.

Who is the boss of me? The invitation to trust God and rest is a way to answer this question. If God is the boss of us (i.e. if we follow His ways) then resting will become a part of the healthy rhythm of our lives. But if He isn't… well, then slavery is most likely more our cup of tea. We become enslaved to whatever we worship.

Resting is part of the Divine Order of God. Maybe it's partly because *rest* is one of the things we can't really control. The Old Testament idea of Jubilee is part of God's design for a nation. Every fifty years all things were to return to the original owners and the land was not to be worked.

They were to party for a whole year. Wow!

No working. No slaves. No debt. Only Jubilee.

But the idea is so foreign to our human programming that the Israelites never, ever did it. Not once. Even though it was ordered by God! Even when they had the best and godliest leaders – no Jubilee.

No resting.

Sound familiar?

Rest may be the last act of God's creative process but it is surely one of the hardest. Light we can handle, expanse we can accept, and foundations we believe in. Simplicity and complexity we will wrestle with and do our best. Life – let's do it! But rest? Really? You can almost hear and feel the sinews in our bodies and our minds cry out: "But there is just so much to do!"

If we think for a while about this concept of rest, we know that things bear more and better fruit when they are rested. People, that's you and me, included.

The challenge is to trust. To believe God and to enter rest. On purpose. With God's help as the master creator. We can call upon Him to help inspire us to believe Him and to take a break. Why not participate with God in the great creative, beautiful mess by choosing to defy slavery and believe God? Take a rest now.

Questions

- Where do you get your value from?

- Do you ever find yourself defining who you are by what you do? What effect is this having on your sense of identity and purpose?

- Would those closest to you say that you are enslaved to your work? How does their response make you feel?

- What are the things that make it difficult for you to value and take rest?

- Is the rhythm of your life determined solely by your work patterns?

- Do you struggle to find rest?

- Does it ever feel like the rest that you take is simply about recovering from your work?

- What do you have to lay aside so that rest becomes an intentional practice in your life?

- How can you help others embrace rest? Do your behaviour and expectations lead others to think that rest isn't important or is a "sign of weakness"?

- Who is the boss of you? How will resting affect this?

- Jesus invites us to come to him "all you who are weary and burdened" and offers us rest. Spend some time focusing on this and taking Jesus at his word.

Conclusion

The way God creates is breathtaking. I'm watching it right now as I track together with some people who have made a new start of their lives. Out of the chaos of their pain, sin, fear, darkness, God spoke and everything began to look different.

It's such a good reminder of my own journey. I could never have guessed God's re-creative work could have been so beautiful. And the work continues.

Why does this matter?

It matters because the way God created the first things are a pattern for the way He re-creates all things. It matters because God is in the business of redeeming and re-creating the world. His plan and pattern is to see His Kingdom come to earth as it is in heaven. It's what He taught us to pray for and work for and long for. And we do.

Every dark place needs to be invaded with light. Every life lost in chaos needs to hear the incredible truth that God is near – just waiting to create new life.

Every time I feel lost and confused and overwhelmed, it is not wasted – it's an opportunity to watch, listen and trust that God has something beautiful in mind. Something new and creative is at work all around us, all the time. If we had eyes to see and ears to hear we could start to imagine what God has in store for those of us who have thrown our lives on Him.

I'm not sure what stage you are in or what pattern you have noticed as you read this book. I seem to be in a perpetual state of re-creation… needing light to see my way (just enough, mind you, to see the way forward – not so much that I'll get freaked out and stop from fear). I need to be reminded not to shrink my world into manageable parts that I can control. God is continuing to pry my fingers apart until I can remain open-handed with all I have and who I am. Living open-handed in a posture of trust is a re-creation that seems almost new every morning. God continues to teach me, by His grace, and I am both simple and complex as I embrace His Truth.

Not only that, but God invites me into a partnership. To re-create with Him. Making the world a more beautiful place. What an invitation! I long for the time when everyone could grasp that invitation. We can be co-creators with God. Not just by having babies (although that's also a fun way to be part of the creation story), but by spreading light and freedom, and expanse and truth and guiding people through seasons and inviting people to be part of this process as well. We get to be a part of this incredible work of beauty – this art called life.

And then we rest. We step back and breathe in the beauty of a love-filled, creative God. A God who uses every shade and vibrancy of colour to re-create our lives in ways we could never have imagined or dreamed. We get to stop working, and celebrate the incredible truth that we are, all of us, a beautiful mess.

Activity

Draw a timeline which identifies times of chaos within your life. As you reflect on each of these, work through the process of the Divine Order moving from chaos to light to expanse to seasons to life to co-creating and finally, to rest. Pay attention to the detail of this.

- What do you notice about the pattern you have identified?

- How did the light dawn in your chaos?

- Who or what brought the light?

- What was the clarity that was revealed?

- How did you respond to this revelation?

Endnotes

1. Genesis 1:1, my paraphrase

2. Thomas Merton, Thoughts in Solitude: (www.goodreads.com/quotes/80913-my-lord-god-i-have-no-idea-where-i-am)

3. Jeremiah 18:6, NIV

4. John 1:5, NLT

5. Acts 9:3, NLT

6. Douglas Coupland, *Life After God*, New York: Scribner, 2002, pp. 289–290

7. Proverbs 29:18, KJV

8. Psalm 1:3, NIV

9. John 10:10, NIV

10. "Bereaved Parents: particular difficulties, unique factors, and treatment issues", *Social Work*, vol. 30, p. 20

11. John 9:1–12

12. Genesis 1:27, NIV

13. see www.amazon.ca/Am-Malala-Stood-Education-Taliban/dp/0316322407)

14. Genesis 4:9, NIV

15. Romans 8:20–22

16. Ralph Neighbour, *The Arrival Kit*, Houston, TX: Touch Outreach Ministries, 2011

17. Matthew 11:28, NIV

THE LIBERATING TRUTH

How Jesus empowers women

Danielle Strickland

"This may be the most significant issue of our time – how Jesus sees females."
Lieut.-Colonel Janet Munn, Secretary for Spiritual Life Development, The Salvation Army

Despite decades of legislation, women are still straitjacketed into subservient roles. Girls still "dumb down" in order to catch a good-looking guy. From Barbies to burqas to Botox, women are offered models which stifle their development.

The Church needs to stand against such practices. Danielle Strickland argues that it should seize the lead in offering women everywhere – especially younger women – new opportunities to develop their talents.

"The Liberating Truth will rock your world!"
Patricia King, Co-founder of XPmedia

"Danielle's passion for the Kingdom of God shines through. A challenging and powerful read for both sexes."
Mike Pilavachi, Soul Survivor

"This book is amazing! Danielle is the living embodiment of its message."
Wendy Beech-Ward, Director of Spring Harvest

ISBN 978 0 85721 019 7 | £7.99 | $12.99

BOUNDLESS

Living life in overflow
Danielle Strickland and Stephen Court

"An encouraging and dynamic exploration of what it means to live the abundant life that Jesus promised. Told through an engaging collection of stories and anecdotes ... Boundless reaches some very deep and challenging places... in [an] accessible, appealing way."
Youthwork magazine

- What if there were ways to live that filled you, rather than depleting you?

- What if there were an ocean of joy, freedom and wholeness within reach?

- What if you could tap into an inexhaustible resource of power and love?

- What would your life look like without fear?

These are the questions God put deep inside of us, so we'd go looking for *more*. Looking for more is what this book is all about – a massive jump into a boundless ocean of love. Take the plunge!

ISBN 978 0 85721 451 5 | £6.99 | $10.99